First Published in Britain 2019
Author: Gill McGregor NDSF CBA Cert Ed.
Designs by: Gill McGregor
Copyright © Gill McGregor 2019
Published by: Gill McGregor College Publishers
ISBN 978-0-9929332-7-2
Volume 1
Printed in the U
Layout design: www.sosb

Trademarks.
All trademarks are acknowledged as belonging to their respective companies.

Limit of Liability and Disclaimer of Warranty.
Whilst every effort has been made to make this book as accurate and complete as possible, the Publisher, the Author or anyone else involved with the preparation of this book accept no liability for the use of the techniques and materials, nor for errors or omissions, or changes that may subsequently be made, variations in colour from original artwork to their reproduction within these pages due to differences in equipment, paper, inks and other conditions.

Introduction

By Gill McGregor

Whilst we strive to maintain the natural ecological balance in the environment through reducing pollution, we are seeking alternative mechanics to support, control and anchor, our plant materials in floral designs.

I have found this to be an exciting assignment which has challenged the very way we arrange our flowers and foliage. The styles of designs we arrange are a consequence of the mechanics we choose to use. The mechanics we choose are often of consequence to the containers we select.

We look to natural and man made materials to create mechanics which satisfy our need to contribute towards preserving the planet and its natural systems and resources.

I have found that many leaf manipulation techniques have the ability to support, control and anchor flowers and foliage in position to form a pleasing design as can be found in my book "How to... Go Greener Flower Arranging, Leaf Manipulation and Cone and Bark Sculptures", Volume One. Yet recycling is a key component of reducing pollution, so with that in mind I have designed a range of mechanics using a variety of readily available Florist products which can be hand made into a mechanic and reused in our floral designs, which very often reflect the mechanics used in the past.

I have learnt that our arrangement skills will frequently require the need for

Introduction

precision cutting rather than further inserting stems ever deeper into floral foam for the desired affect. We need to defoliate stems meticulously to prevent bacterial damage where the stems are below the water level. We need to consider the potential damage a mechanic can do to the plant material whilst it supports, controls and anchors the materials in position. I now fully appreciate the skills of past floral designers who had no floral foam to use yet created aesthetically pleasing designs.

I hope these mechanics, with practice, will help all floral designers, floral art teachers, demonstrators and florists fulfil your design requirements whilst going greener. Enjoy.

Radial Rustic Wire Armature

To arrange a radial design this simple semicircular armature, when pot taped to the inside of a container, can support the tallest placements of flowers and foliage whilst the mass of foliage extending just above the rim of the container controls and supports the lower placements.

Radial Rustic Wire Armature

P7

To make this rustic wire semicircular armature, cut 2 metres of rustic wire (steel wire encased in rustic twine) and measure one metre to find the centre.

Place a rolling pin in the middle of the wire length and bring the 2 wires around the rolling pin together with the wire nearest you on top of the other wire. Hold the wires as close to the rolling pin as possible. Now twist the rolling pin all the way round in a clockwise direction to make a secure circular wire shape.

Slide the rolling pin out of the newly formed rustic wire circle and place the rolling pin against the splayed wires, adjacent to the circle. Repeat by bringing the 2 wires around the rolling pin together with the wire nearest to you on top and twist the rolling pin once all the way round in the same direction, clockwise, to make the second circular shape.

Repeat using the same method to make a chain of 10 circles. The secret is to ensure you twist the rolling pin in the same direction each time and that the crossing wires are opposite the twist before - so that all the twisted wire is parallel with each other.

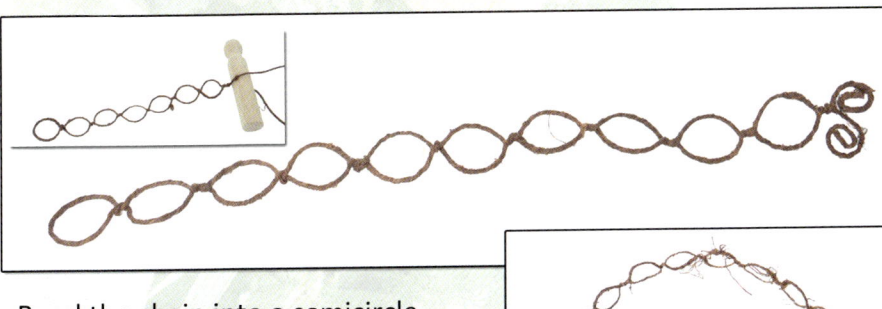

Bend the chain into a semicircle and create coils with the remaining wire for effect.

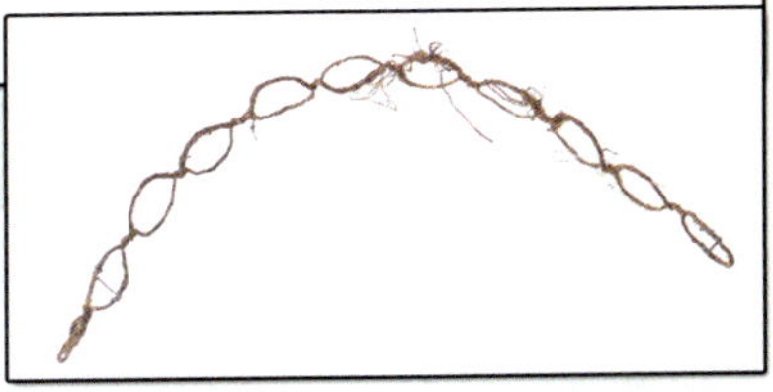

Radial Rustic Wire Armature

P8

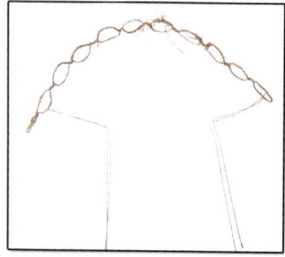 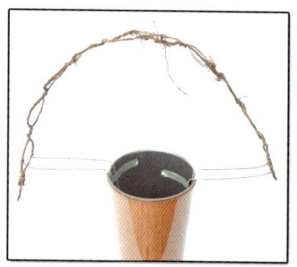 

Using 4 x 1.00mm x 40cm wires secure 2 wires circa 3cms apart at the base of each outer wire circle. Select a clean, dry vase and measure the length of wire that is required to extend outwards at 90 degrees from the rustic wire semicircle and then bend the wire at 90 degrees to rest against either side of the vase. Cut the wire lengths if necessary and tape to the inside of the dry vase with 12 mm pot tape.

Remember; no foliage should remain on any stem, which when arranged, will be below the waterline.

Radial Rustic Wire Armature

P9

The Pittosporum tobira with its large rosette of leaves are positioned densely above the rim of the vase to support the remaining lower placements.

This arrangement of Rosa 'Miss Piggy' has each of the 10 , precision cut, tallest rose placements threaded through the rustic wire circles with Asparagus densiflorus 'Myersii' (foxtail fern) to help fill the armature circles to create this radial design.

Pot Tape Grid

P10

I have used a grid of 12 mm pot tape to cross over the top of a dry, cheap vase to create sufficient yet different sized holes to suit my previously designed arrangement.
A horizontal layer of pot tape was secured, just below the rim, over the ends of the tape which flow down the sides of the vase for extra security.

Pot Tape Grid

P11

Note the front right hole is larger than any other space. This was to ensure that the stems of the concentric ringed Anemone posy hand tied framed with a

Hedera (ivy) collar had sufficient space for insertion through the pot tape grid.

The vase was covered with a table mat to improve the visual appearance of the design and to provide additional lines of movement.

Aluminium Wire Domed Circle with Pin Holder

P12 In order to arrange this design a pin holder was placed underneath a hand made, circular, domed, aluminium structured mechanic, made to size, to fit in the well of the shallow, glass dish.

The pin holder was used to support the tall placements of the heavy Sansevieria (Mother-in law's tongue), Rosa (roses) and ting ting to achieve the height.

To make the domed, circular aluminium structure, create a circle with the aluminium wire, to fit in the well. Do not cut the wire.

Tightly bind the aluminium wire around the circle to achieve greater strength and integrity.

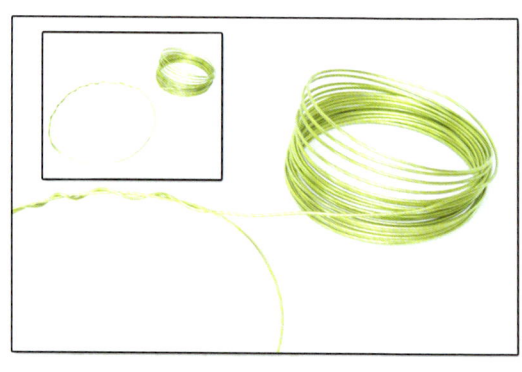

Do not cut the wire.

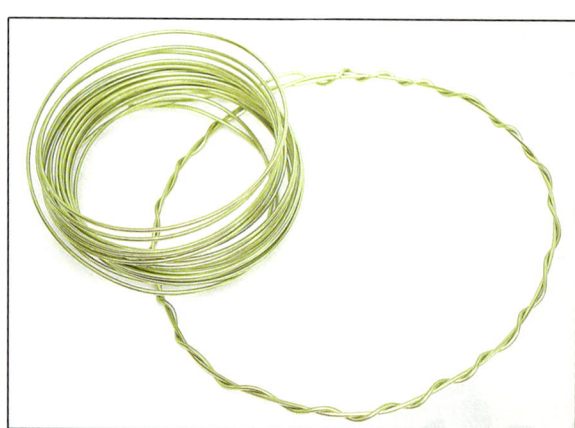

To create the inner coils, use a 2cm diameter plastic test tube or piece of dowel and wind the wire around the cylindrical form one way and then slide out the test tube and

Aluminium Wire Domed Circle with Pin Holder

P13

then wind the wire around the test tube the opposite way and slide out the test tube.
Repeat to create a length of wire circles in opposing directions.

Do not cut the wire but start to position the length of circles to create a domed shape inside the ring, by bringing it across from one side to the other whilst wrapping it around the outer circle and locking the circles into

position by threading them through adjacent circles to make a secure, circular, domed mesh. You may find you will need to make more circular chain in order to form a domed structure which is sufficiently strong to support low placements. When happy with your structure cut the wire and finish with a spiral loop.

For this design a 20cm (8 inch) diameter domed structure was made using 7.5m of aluminium wire.

Aluminium Wire Domed Circle with Pin Holder

P14

The joy of this aluminium mechanic is that; the circles can be squeezed together to make sure all materials are supported where needed. This mechanic can be recycled and reused and the wire domed structure can be a feature within a design due to its attractive, aesthetic look.

Additional strands of opposing circle wires can be incorporated in the design for unity.

This design includes manipulated Rhapis exalta (finger palm, lady palm) as sculptured, rolled and single puff forms to aid visual interest. Their light weight stems are threaded through the aluminium mechanic for support and anchorage.

Aluminium Wire Domed Circle with Pin Holder

P15

Stacked Cornus Square Grid

Cut 12 dry Cornus sticks to measure 33cms.

If using freshly cut Cornus allow the stems to dry out for 2 weeks before construction otherwise the wiring will become loose when the fresh twigs dehydrate and therefore shrink.

Place 2 sticks horizontally 25cms apart and stack two more sticks vertically on top to form a 25cm square with an overhang of 5cms. Using paper covered or metallic wire, lash the sticks together by binding securely to create a cross pattern, before twisting the wires together to finish on the underside of the structure and cut the residue wire.

Repeat stacking pairs of sticks alternately towards the centre binding to secure each pair to produce a slightly raised grid in the centre.

Individually bend 4 x 90mm x 40cm green lacquered wires to create a hook at the tip.

Hook each wire circa 15cms apart, where 2 sticks cross, so the long wires become a handle underneath the grid and twist to secure.

Stacked Cornus Square Grid

P17

Spiral the wires at the centre and then twist 4 times to secure together, thus making a handle.

I have used 10 Rosa, 3 Fatsia japonica leaves, 3 stems of Cupressus and 3 of fir and removed any foliage which I believe will be below the grid. Wire 3 fir cones, 5 baubles and orange slices.

Stacked Cornus Square Grid

P18

Arrange by threading the flowers and foliage from the centre of the grid outwards as desired, whilst spiralling the stems. Remember the centre placements should be slightly taller to create a domed profile. Add the cones, baubles and slices for effect and poke their wire ends back up into the design so they cannot be seen.

Stacked Cornus Square Grid

P19

Check all stems below the grid are removed of leaves and thorns before placing the 3 Fatsias underneath the grid to help frame the design and give added depth. Tie with string to secure and disguise with 12mm green pot tape. Cut the stems at a 45 degree angle to your desired length and place in a clean vase of water. Finish with a metre length of beaded baubles which are woven and threaded through the Cornus stacked grid and secured each end with decorative wire.

Circular Rustic Wire Mechanic...

P20

To make this rustic wire structure as an alternative mechanic to floral foam, cut 5.25 metres of rustic wire (steel wire encased in rustic twine) and measure 2.625 metres to find the centre.

Place a rolling pin in the middle of the wire length and bring the 2 wires around the rolling pin together with the wire nearest you on top of the other wire. Hold the wires as close to the rolling pin as possible. Now twist the rolling pin all the way round in a clockwise direction to make a secure circular wire shape.

Slide the rolling pin out of the newly formed rustic wire circle and place the rolling pin against the splayed wires, adjacent to the circle. Repeat by bringing the 2 wires around the rolling pin together to create a second tight round circular shape and twist the rolling pin once all the way round in the same direction to secure.

Repeat using the same method to make a chain of 11 circles. The secret is to ensure you twist the rolling pin in the same direction each time.

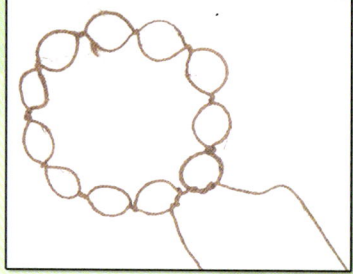

Bend the chain into a circle and secure with the remaining wire. Do not cut the 2 wires. Complete by making an open, secure mesh like structure by fashioning one of the lengths of wire, by hand, into a similar shaped circle and secure to an existing circle by winding the wire around

...with Woven Typha

twice before moving on to form the next circle, repeat to make a total of 6 circles. Repeat making additional circles with the other wire length in the opposite direction.
With the residue wire make a mesh in the centre before securing the wire ends together.

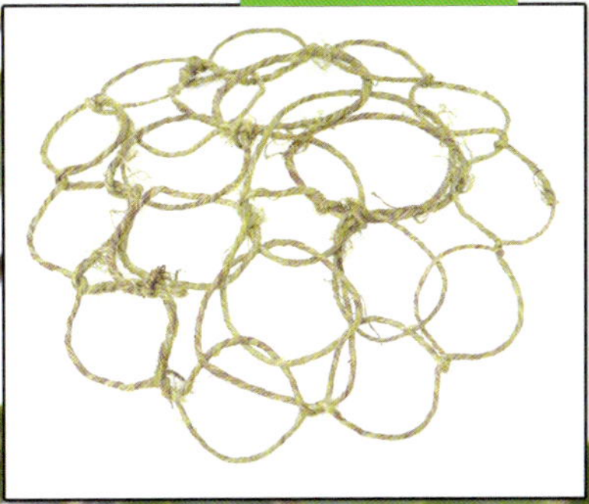

P21

Circular Rustic Wire Mechanic...

Weave 10 Typha blades of grass to form loops through the rustic wire open mesh structure. Always insert each blade upwards from the middle of the structure so all 10 blade ends are centrally below the structure to help to actually balance the design. Alternatively floppy, split Phormium tenax can be used.

Finish by arranging your selected flowers, foliage and seed heads through the rustic wire structure with threaded Typha for effect with stems spiralling. Tie the stems securely to hold in position with jute string and disguise with 12mm green pot tape. Make sure all the stems are clean, below the tying point, before cutting the stems at a 45 degree angle to the desired length and place the completed design in a clean vase of water.

...with Woven Typha

P23

Heart Frame

P24

One reel of diamond cut wire has been used to make this attractive heart shaped mechanic suitable for vase or wedding designs.

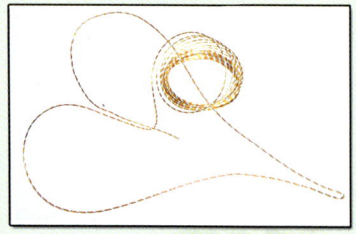

Measure 10cms of wire to create a handle, before bending the diamond cut wire from what will be the base of the cleavage into a heart shape with a long point. Do not cut the wire.

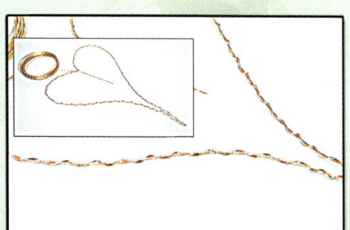

Continue to bind around the heart shape uniformly to strengthen the structure. Do not cut the wire.

Commence bending the wire into random sized circles to create an attractive, open, domed mesh.

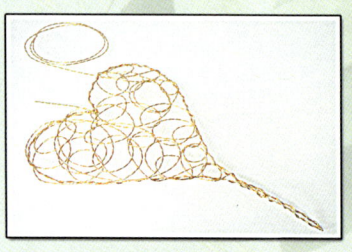

By winding the wire around the outline shape and locking the circles through each other you can make the structure hold itself together without using additional securing methods.

Finish with the end of the wire to form another handle.

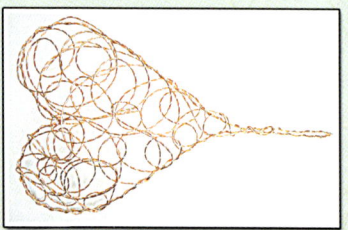

If making the mechanic for a bridal bouquet it is best not to use additional wires to secure the "open" heart into position in case the ends of the wire damage the dress.

Heart Frame

P25

A posy of Rosa 'Avalanche' with natural stems, framed with Ruscus hypoglossum (hard ruscus) has been threaded through the heart shaped mechanic to make this wedding bouquet. The handle finished as appropriate.

Heart Frame

P26

This delightful wedding bouquet uses wired Rosa 'Avalanche' brought through the centre of the heart mechanic for effect.

Heart Frame

P27

This heart shaped vase with a diagonal aperture evidences the heart frame mechanic to support the Phalaenopsis orchids and Craspedia globosa. The dark green Fatsia japonica leaf was positioned underneath the heart to highlight this aesthetically attractive mechanic. Dracaena fragrans were positioned in the glass vase to hide the stems and to support a single Phalaenopsis flower in the water.

Wire Armature for Vertical Designs

P28   This wire armature for a cylindrical vase is a superb give away mechanic.

Use 5 x 1.5mm x 50cm green lacquered wires to make a circle at the top of each wire by winding the wires tip around a 2cm diameter plastic test tube or dowel. Bend each loop to be at a 90 degree angle to the wire length.

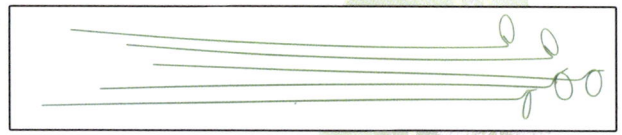

Take 1 x 0.90mm x 50cm green lacquered wire and wind twice around an empty wine bottle to achieve a curved wire and make the circle to be the same size as the aperture of the vase and secure by winding the residue wire around the circular wire.

Stagger the wire loops as required to echo how you arrange a vertical design with variation of rhythmic movement.

Find the end of the wire for the tallest loop and measure 5cms up from the tallest looped wire base.

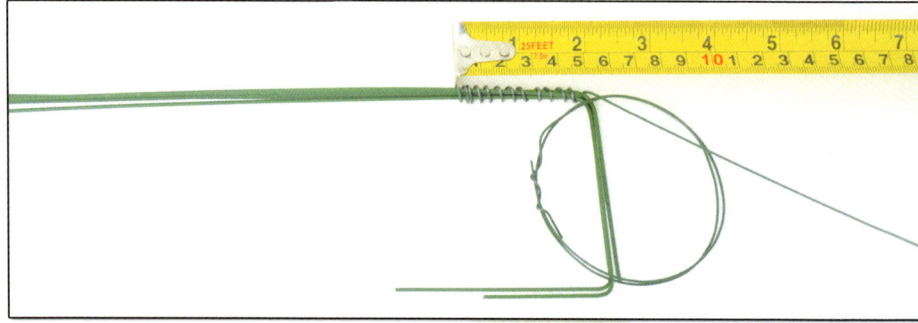

Bind the 5 wires together with a 0.90mm x 50cm green lacquered wire downwards for 5cms to the tallest loops wire end. Do not cut the wire. Bend the 4 remaining 1.5mm wires beyond the bound wire area at a 90 degree angle to form a base.

Wire Armature for Vertical Designs

P29

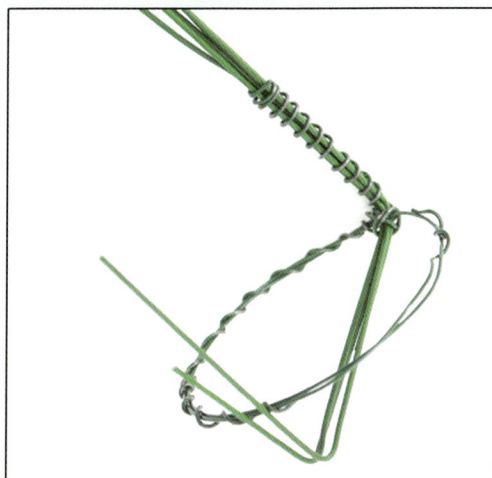

Take the 0.90mm circle you have made and place against the nook of the bent wires and lash twice with the uncut 0.90mmm wire and continue to bind the residue around the circle. Position the base wires to be in the middle of the 0.90mm circular and bend the wire tips upwards at a 90 degree angle.

Secure with an additional 0.90mm x 50cm green lacquered wire by lashing the wires to the circle and continue to bind the remaining wire around the circle for extra stability.

Place the structure in the vase and thread plant materials through the armature to your desired lengths.

Wire Armature for Vertical Designs

P30

Filler foliage placed in close order to protrude just above the rim will prevent the armature wobbling. Further materials can then be arranged for effect.

Wire Armature for Vertical Designs

P31

The vase housing this design measures 31cms tall with an aperture of 7cms diameter. Alliums were precision cut to size and 2 placements were threaded through each loop. The remaining materials were then arranged through a mass of foliage protruding just above the rim of the vase to prevent the armature from moving.

A midolino "Swan's neck" was incorporated to aid distinction.

"Z" Shaped Cornus Frame

P32

This give away mechanic is made with dried Cornus and aluminium wire which allows for a contemporary arrangement of 20 Dianthus (carnations) to be threaded through the "Z" shaped aluminium wire to create diagonal lines of movement. Filler materials at the base support the structure to make it stable and provide textural contrast.

To give it away, the design is carefully removed from the vase and the stems are tied with string to hold them together.

For a vase 30cms tall with an aperture of 20cms x 4cms, I have cut 2 x 90cm lengths of dried Cornus. If your vase is different in height, cut to create the visual height you require. Cut 2 x 20cm additional lengths of Cornus or of a suitable width to fit in your selected vase. Cross lash horizontally each 20cm Cornus length with paper covered wire 20cms apart and 5cms from each stem end for support. The cross lashed stems are hidden in the vase.

"Z" Shaped Cornus Frame

P33

Using circa 180cms-250cms of aluminium wire, leave a small amount of residue wire and secure the aluminium wire to one vertical Cornus stem 10cms above the top horizontal strut and bring the wire diagonally across and wind round the other vertical Cornus stem before leading it back diagonally to continue forming an even "Z" shape bound in position.
Do not cut the wire.

Do make sure that the top diagonal of the aluminium wire's positioning allows for the length of the top carnation stem being able to be in water.

For my vase height I have spaced the diagonal lines to be 25cms apart.

Repeat by bringing the aluminium wire downwards and binding the wire to echo the "Z" shape ensuring there is space between the aluminium wires to thread the carnations through. Finish by coiling the wire ends for effect.

"Z" Shaped Cornus Frame

P34

Once the mechanic is placed in a vase thread the carnation stems through the 2 diagonal wires starting at the top with the stems all parallel with each other to create a further contrast of vertical line.

"Z" Shaped Cornus Frame

P35

The wires can be squashed closer together to ensure the carnations stay in position. Cut the vertical Cornus to the required height and complete the design as desired.

Aluminium Wire Circular Grid

P36

A wonderful reusable aluminium mechanic used not only to support flowers but can be an intricate part of the overall design.

Using the same construction method shown on pages 12 to 13. *My selected vase measures 24cms tall with an aperture of 14cms. I therefore made my domed mechanic to measure 21cms in diameter, half again larger in diameter than the aperture, for visual balance.*

Using aluminium wire, make a circle 21cms in diameter or to a suitable size to suit your selected vase. Do not cut the wire. Continue winding the reel of aluminium wire to bind around the circle securely and uniformly to provide greater strength and integrity. Do not cut the wire.

Using a 2cm diameter plastic test tube or piece of dowel wind the wire around the cylindrical form one way and then slide out the test tube and then wind the wire around the tube the opposite way and repeat to create a length of wire circles in opposing directions.

Don't cut the wire but position the length of circles to create a domed shape inside the circle, by wrapping it around the circle and locking the circles into position by threading them through adjacent

Aluminium Wire Circular Grid

P37

wire circles to make a secure, circular, domed mesh. You may find you will need to make more circular chain in order to form a domed structure which is sufficiently strong to support low placements. When happy with your structure, cut the wire and finish with a spiral loop. Different colours of aluminium wire can aid distinction.

Rest the completed mechanic on the rim of the vase asymmetrically for effect. Commence arranging your materials by adding a precision cut, strong backbone of foliage with blunt cut stems to hold the mechanic in to your desired position, the stems will rest flat on the vase's base for greater stability. Ensure all the stems are defoliated where in the water. You will need to precision cut each placement before arranging by threading through your aluminium wire circular grid. **This mechanic can facilitate both traditional and contemporary designs.**

A super mechanic for contract work or as a gift.

To note the use of this mechanic allows for the arranged design to be removed from the vase carefully whilst incorporating the mechanic/plant materials and tied with string to hold the stems into position in order to be given away.

Aluminium Wire Rectangular Frame

P38

This curved, rectangular, aluminium mechanic provides the support for tall arrangements to be constructed. The precision cut, backbone foliage helps to hold the structure in to position, as they are threaded through the looped wires. Their stems must touch the bottom of the vase to ensure stability.

The construction method is the same as the aluminium circle domed mesh (page 36-37), except it is made to be rectangular in shape.

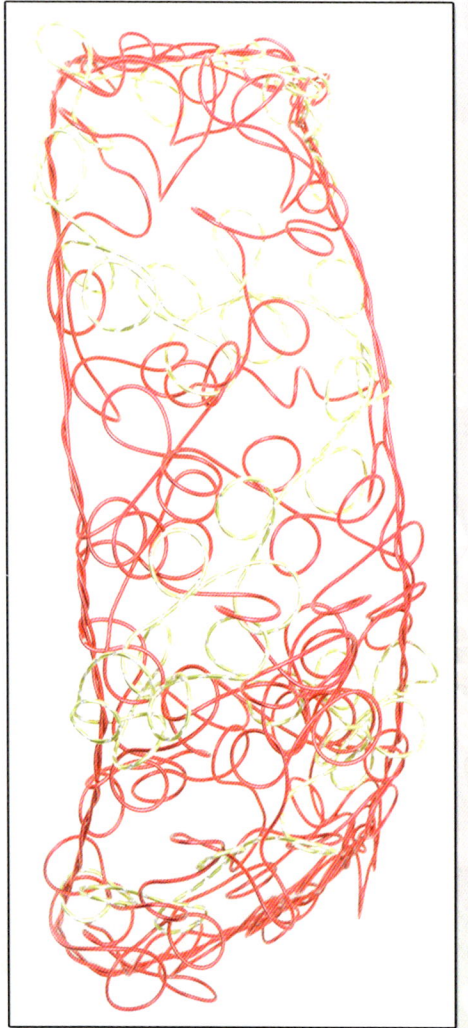
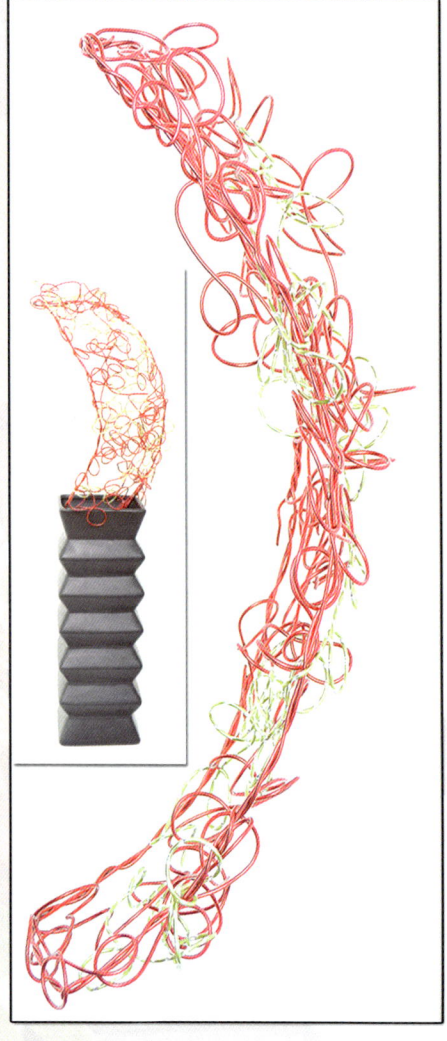

Aluminium Wire Rectangular Frame

P39

To arrange the design, precision cut plant materials are threaded through the structure for control and support. Filler materials arranged just above the vase's rim also help to support placements.

For the size of my design I used, in total, the equivalent of one whole reel (11.5m x 2mm) of aluminium wire interspersed with a contrasting wire for effect.

Aluminium Wire Rectangular Frame

P40

Aluminium Wire Rectangular Frame

P41

The entire design can be removed from the vase and tied in place to give away if performing a floral art demonstration.

The Hazards of Using Chicken Wire as a Mechanic.

Scrunched up chicken wire wedged in a container with water may not be the best solution to arranging flowers and foliage as an alternative to using floral foam.

Why, you may ask?

The nature of the scrunched chicken wire is rough, the gaps between the wire are not uniform as the spaces may be very close together which whilst aiding stability can also potentially result in injuring the stems as the plant material is pushed through the chicken wire.

Why is this a problem?

When a stem is wounded, when a leaf is ripped or a petal or leaf bruised—it will emit ethylene as a stress response.

What is ethylene?

Ethylene is an odourless, colourless gas hormone produced within the tissues of plants as part of their natural life cycle to stimulate normal life processes of development and maturation and is released into the atmosphere. Natural ethylene producers include; apples, avocados, bananas, cantaloupe melons, kiwis, peaches, pears, peppers and tomatoes. It is also present in everyday life from non-natural sources, including combustion engines, propane heaters and cigarette smoke.

What does ethylene do?

Its overall effect on plant material is that it stimulates ripening, wilting, and decay of plants and plant products (flowers, fruit and vegetables).

What effect has ethylene gas on flowers?

Exposure to ethylene gas can cause: bud and leaf abscission (falling off), leaf yellowing or leaf transparency, loss of deep colour, flower or petal drop, irregular bud opening and premature death.

But why is chicken wire a potential issue?

If a stem is damaged when arranged in chicken wire, the

The Hazards of Using Chicken Wire as a Mechanic.

P43

injured stem will emit ethylene gas as a stress response, thus raising the level of ethylene in the atmosphere which results in damage/ the premature death of that flower or foliage and if not removed from the design will then cause the damage/ premature death of the plant material in close proximity.

Food for thought.

We also have to appreciate that when Chicken Wire was first used, central heating was less common and homes in general were cooler. But today most households have central heating and plants and flowers not only produce more ethylene at higher temperatures, but they are more sensitive to ethylene damage at high temperatures too, which will effect the longevity and quality of the materials used in the design.

A typical instruction from a Flower Arranging Book in the period that preceded Floral Foam might read:
'always aim to get four or five layers of netting in an upright vase'

The chicken wire mechanics used to create the design on page 45; and the damage it has done to so many stems.

The Hazards of Using Chicken Wire as a Mechanic.

P44

Are some flowers more sensitive to ethylene?

Yes, flowers exhibit varying degrees of ethylene sensitivity. Here is a list of flowers which are ethylene sensitive:

Achillea, Aconitum, Agapanthus, Alchemilla, Allium, Alstroemeria, Anethum, Antirrhinum, Aquilegia, Asclepias, Astilbe, Astrantia, Bouvardia, Brodiaea, Campanula, Celosia, Centaurea, Chamelaucium, Chelone, Consolida, Cymbidium, Crocosmia, Daucus carota, Delphinium, Dendrobium, Dianthus, Dianthus dealbata, Dicentra, Doronicum, Echium, Eremurus, Eustoma, Freesia, Francoa, Gladiolus, Godetia, Gypsophila, Helianthus, Ixia, Kniphofia, Lathyrus, Lavatera, Lilium, Limonium, Lysimachia, Matthiola, Phlox, Physostegia, Ranunculus, Rosa (not all), Rudbeckia, Saponaria, Scabiosa, Silene, Solidaster, Trachelium, Trollius, Veronica.

Some simple rules to aid plant material longevity;

Handle plant material with care to prevent bruising/ damage.
Cut plant material using clean, sharp implements.
Cut stems at a 45 degree angle to open up the surface area which absorbs water.
Remove damaged leaves and petals.
Remove the lower leaves which will be below the water level.
If a lateral stem is broken- do not leave a jagged wound, cut to create a clean cut.
As flowers age remove dying or older flowers.
Do not store flowers in bud with older, mature flowers.
Store flowers in a cool, well ventilated place unless they particularly need a warmer environment.
Botrytis and other fungi that degrade dying plant material produce their own ethylene, so ensure there is good ventilation and remove flowers and foliage which display signs of fungal damage.
Never place flowers near fruit and vegetables.

The Hazards of Using Chicken Wire as a Mechanic.

P45

Avoid placing flowers where they will be exposed to heavy cigarette smoke, exhaust fumes and propane heaters. Do not place flowers near a heat source or in a hot environment.
Change the water everyday to prevent bacterial build up in the water and stem ends. Select mechanics which do not damage the plant materials.

Raised Ring Grid

P46

This layered wreath ring mechanic aids stability to anchor heavier plant materials as there are 2 aluminium wire grids with space between to provide greater support and control of your arranged materials.

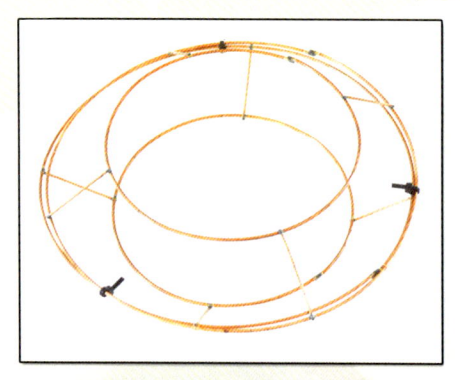

Cable tie the outer rings of 2 x 20cm (8 inches) raised wire rings together, equidistant apart with 3 Cable ties.

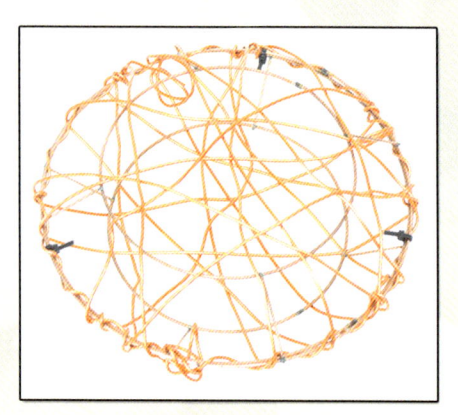

This bound wire will help prevent the constructed grids from moving.

Spiral the end of the aluminium wire and again secure to the outer edge and then wrap the wire around the raised copper rings to create a random 3 dimensional grid. Intermittently bind the wire around the outer edge to prevent the wire from moving. This loose mesh allows the stems to be inserted through the edges, top and base of the structure.

Using aluminium wire, create a spiral coil before securing to the cable tied frames at the widest point and bind around the outer edge. Cut the wire and finish with a coil.

Raised Ring Grid

P47

This design evidences a precision cut Dracaena 'Green tie' collar with each stem stripped cleaned where the stems are in water. With recessed Cupressus & Ceanothus to act as a supporting filler.

Raised Ring Grid

P48

Raised Ring Grid

P49

Precision cut Leucadendron 'Safari sunset' act as the backbone to aid stability, whilst Rosa 'Peach avalanche' are arranged to provide an open design with profile.

Triangular Frame of Cornus and . . .

P50

Heavier weighted flowers and foliage need greater support to anchor the plant material into your desired vase.

For a vase measuring 35 cms tall with an aperture of 10 cms diameter I have made a dried Cornus Asymmetrical triangle with measurement of 95cms x 65cms x 45cms securely bound lashed with metallic wire to hold in to position. Additional diagonal struts of dried Cornus have been attached, bound with metallic wire to secure, to further strengthen the Cornus structure.

Lengths of colour coordinated aluminium wires were wound around a 2cm diameter plastic tube or dowel to create long spiralled wire coils which were attached to the Cornus asymmetrical frame to create diagonal lines of movement and to become the supports for plant materials to be threaded through when arranging.

...Spiralled Aluminium Wire

P51

Once the completed framework is placed in the vase, precision cut Protea, with clean, defoliated stems, have been threaded through the Cornus and aluminium wire structure for support and control. A smaller Cornus and aluminium wire asymmetrical framework together with a premade circular spiral ring have also been incorporated into this design. Rolled Dracaena fragrans have been arranged to achieve greater distinction.

The Cornus structure is visible for additional effect.

Coiled Aluminium Ring with . . .

P52

This coiled ring made from aluminium wire requires 3 times the diameter of the completed circle worth of spiralled aluminium wire to be moulded into a circular shape and joined together for effect. The more coils of aluminium wire added, the stronger the coil and the closer the spaces are between. For example a circle whose diameter is 10cms requires a coiled length to measure 30cms before bending and securing into a circular, coiled ring.

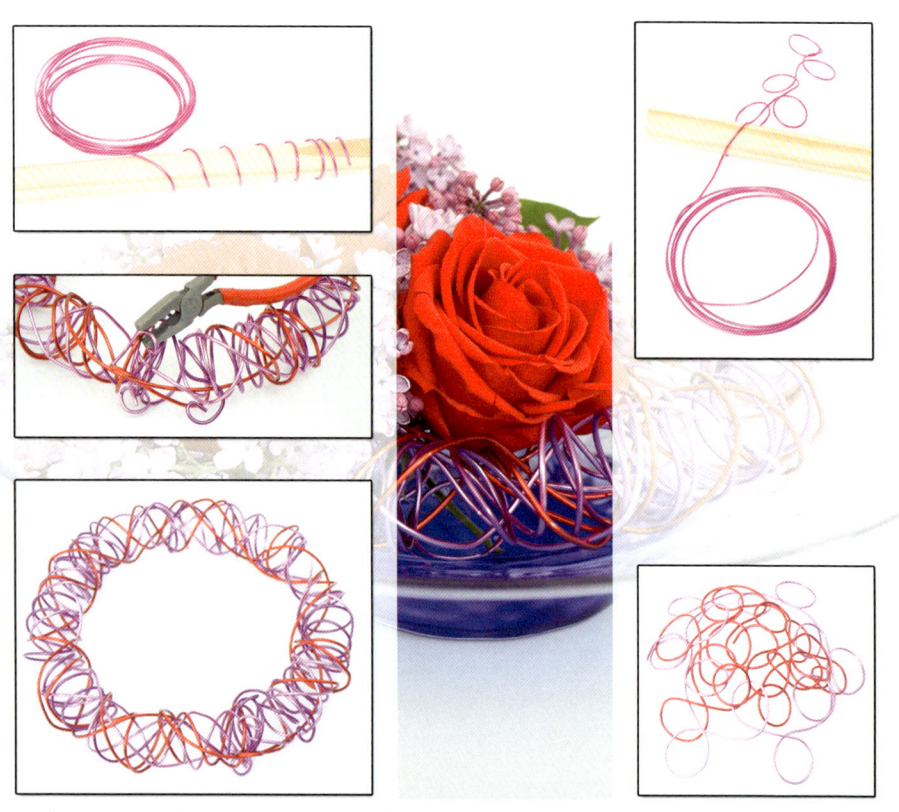

Take a 3cm diameter piece of dowel and wind your selected aluminium wire around the required length of dowel which has been measured and marked to ensure your correct length is produced. Continue to add different coloured aluminium wires until you feel the spaces between are of sufficient size to support your selected plant materials.

...Domed Aluminium Mechanic

P53

To create this Domed Aluminium Mechanic the same sized dowel is used and aluminium wire is wound round to create a circle before it is slipped off the dowel and the wire is then wound in the opposite direction to create a further circular shape. Repeat winding the wire to create circles in opposing direction until you have sufficient to knit together by threading wire circles through each other to make an open domed mesh slightly larger than the diameter of the coiled ring. Place the open mesh aluminium mechanic on top of the coiled ring positioned in your selected dish before arranging your selected plant materials.

This design of Syringa vulgaris (lilac), stripped of most of its' foliage is enhanced with 3 Rosa (rose) 'Freedom' to provide a simple coffee table design. Part of the coiled circle ring is visible for greater distinction.

Square Aluminium Wire Armature

P54

For an alternative outline shape why not make a square?

Aluminium wire wound round a plastic test tube to form a 16 holed square armature allows for 1 x 20 bunch of Dianthus (carnations) threaded through to make a long lasting design.

Square Aluminium Wire Armature

P55

Using 275cms of green aluminium wire and a 3cm diameter plastic test tube or dowel, place the test tube in the middle of the wire length and bring the 2 wires together to form a tight round shape around the test tube. Hold the wires as close to the test tube with the wire closest to you on top and twist the test tube twice in the same direction to secure.

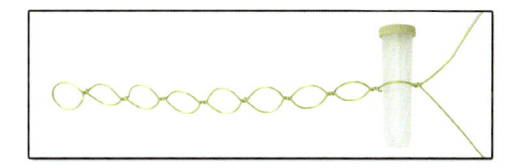

Repeat using the same method to make a chain of 16 circles. The secret is to ensure you twist the test tube in the same direction each time.

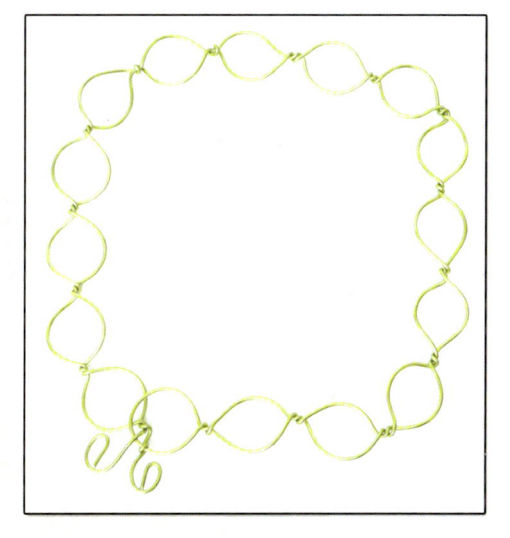

Slide the test tube out of the newly formed aluminium wire circle and place the test tube against the splayed wires, adjacent to the circle. Bring the 2 wires together to create a second tight round shape encasing the test tube, with the wire nearest to you on top and twist the test tube twice in the same direction to secure.

Bend the chain into a square and secure with the remaining wire into position before bending the excess wire into flat spirals for effect.

Square Aluminium Wire Armature

P56

Clean the stems of all the materials to be used in the design which will be in water. Thread 16 carnations through each of the holes so they are hung by their heads. Holding the stems, carefully turn the threaded heads upside down so the flower heads slightly rest on your work table and spiral the stems.

Face to make a front facing design by manoeuvring the carnations to be up at the back and down at the front before bind tying into position with jute string.

Manipulate 4 x Aspidistra elatior leaves into knots to become additional mechanics (see pages 66 - 69 of How to... Go Greener Flower Arranging, Leaf Manipulation and Cone and Bark Sculptures) and

Square Aluminium Wire Armature

P57

arrange inside the carnation square collar before arranging the remaining 4 carnations through the knotted Aspidistra for support to provide a square pattern inside. Add textured foliage such as Asparagus pyramidalis (tree fern) for contrast.

Complete the design by adding 5 x looped Aspidistra at the front of the square as a collar and bind tie with jute string before disguising with 12mm pot tape and place in a textured, water filled vase.

Crescent Aluminium Frame

P58

This crescent shaped mechanic is made by making an "eye" shaped outline to your desired size with aluminium wire before binding around the outline with the wire to provide additional strength. Complete by making chains of opposing aluminium circles (see pages 13-16) using the same method in your selected colours and wind them around the eye shape before locking the circles through each other for greater stability. Curve the design to your desired crescent shape.

Remember to make sure you have a few wires coming down from the centre to make a handle you can hold.

Crescent Aluminium Frame

P59

The secret of making this crescent shaped design is to weave soft pliable foliage through the structure making sure the clean stem ends are positioned below the design centrally and tie with jute string to secure.

The Crescent structure can then be placed in a vase and cleaned stems threaded through, precision cut, to complete the overall design. This design can be lifted out of the vase and tied with jute string to give as a raffle prize during a demonstration.

Circular Open Rustic Wire Armature

P60

To make this rustic wire open circular armature, cut 2.4 metres of rustic wire (steel wire encased in rustic twine) and measure 1.2 metres to find the centre. Continue to make 12 circles using the same method as the radial mechanic structure page (6).

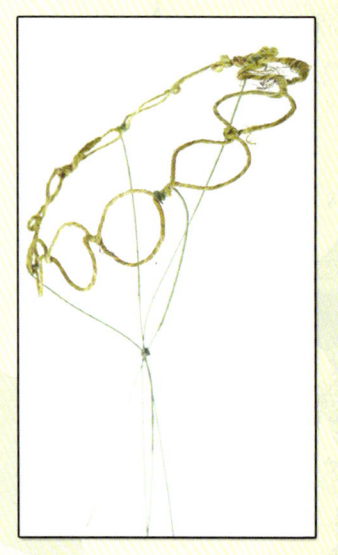

circle, equidistant apart to form handles. Face to make a diagonal armature, up at the back and down at the front.

Defoliate all the stems which you believe will be in water.
Thread 12 Rosa 'Avalanche' through each of the holes and spiral the stems and secure with jute string. Bend the wire handles up from the binding point so the wires will not be in water and cut to be just above the binding point.

Tape together, with green stem tape, 2 x 71mm x 50cm green lacquered wires and repeat to make a total of 4 taped wires and secure to the rustic wire

Circular Open Rustic Wire Armature

P61

Circular Open Rustic Wire Armature

P62

Thread 6 Hypericum and 6 Alchemilla mollis (Lady's mantle) through the spiralled rose stems in position making sure their stems spiral and that they do not extend beyond the circle of roses. Arrange a central focal rose with 3 additional roses, equidistant apart, to radiate around the focal rose to create an overall domed shape. The filler materials will help to support the roses into position. Bind the stems to secure with jute string and cover the string with 12mm green pot tape.

Circular Open Rustic Wire Armature

P63

Place the design in a suitable vase.

Fruit Net Mechanic

P64

I have found that the net bag which holds lemons and limes from the supermarket can be used as a grid when stretched over the aperture of the vase and secured with 12mm clear pot tape. The design can be arranged with all plant material stems' cleaned where they will be in the water and precision cut (so their stems touch the bottom of the vase when arranged) and threaded through the mesh for support and anchorage.

You may find the net starts to "sink" the more you thread through but with care it will stay intact for the duration of the design's construction.

Fruit Net Mechanic

P65

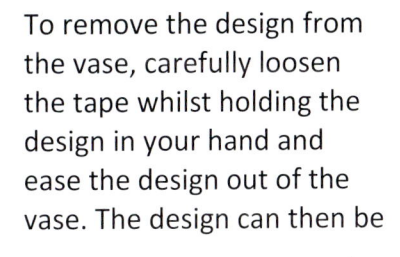

To remove the design from the vase, carefully loosen the tape whilst holding the design in your hand and ease the design out of the vase. The design can then be tied to secure in position with jute string, where the net bag is, with minimal alteration. Disguise the string with 12mm pot tape.

Threaded Carnations

P66

Dianthus (carnations) with cleaned stems, can be threaded through the calyx, parallel to the tips of the green sepals, with aluminium wire. Ensure there is circa 10cms of wire extending beyond the threaded carnations at each end. Carnations are treated with Silver Thiosulfate after harvesting, which acts as an ethylene inhibitor, which means they can withstand the "torture" of being threaded with aluminium wire.

Threaded Carnations

P67

Once threaded carefully curve the threaded carnations to form a circle and secure with the residue aluminium wire. Gather the stems together and turn the carnations upside down and hold so their heads just touch the table. Carefully spiral their stems by selecting a stem and them crossing each consecutive stem over the selected stems the same way. When all have been crossed they will be spiralled, turn the carnations the correct way up.

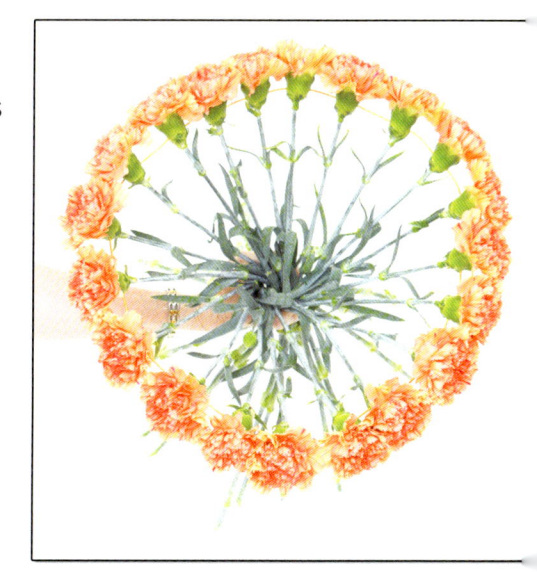

Threaded Carnations

P68

Face the carnation circle if desired to be up at the back and down at the front before securely tying into position with jute string. You can now arrange your selected flowers to be within the carnation circle as a hand tied with stems spiralling and then the stems are cut to your desired length.

Or, you can cut the stems of the tied circle carnation structure, to suit your selected vase, and then place the tied structure in the vase and arrange the remaining flowers through the stems for effect.

Threaded Carnations

P69

This technique can also allow you to make different outline shapes with the threaded carnations.

Aluminium Wire Sphere

P70

This aluminium sphere sits in the neck of a vase which has a tapered rim or can be "hung" with crossed wires going through the sphere over the rim of your vase.

Burst the balloon to remove.

Take thin, short, colour coordinated cable ties and cable tie the wires strategically to make a secure spherical shape.

Do not cut the cable tie ends but weave them through the aluminium wire.

Inflate a latex balloon to the required size and knot. Wind Aluminium wire around the inflated balloon until you feel the wire structure is sufficient to be able to support your plant material. Cut the wire and bend both ends into small spirals.

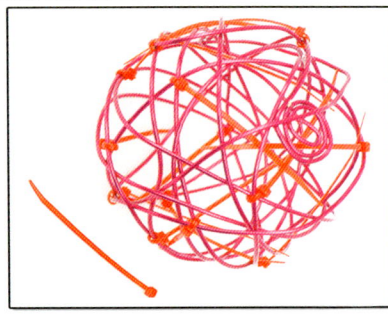

The cable ties are not cut to ensure there are no sharp plastic edges.

Aluminium Wire Sphere

P71

Place the sphere in the tapered neck of the vase and arrange your precision cut back bone flowers or foliage through the sphere, which will support the arranged materials into position.

You may find the sphere moves but once you arrange filler foliage, with cleaned stems low down, through the sphere and around the edges of the rim it will stop moving.

You will now be able to complete your design as required.

Aluminium Wire Sphere

P72

This mechanic is also useful for floral art demonstrations, as the completed design can be removed from the vase with the mechanic and the stems tied into position with jute string just below the sphere as a give away arrangement.

Index

Aluminium Wire Circular Grid	36 to 37
Aluminium Wire Domed Circle with Pin Holder	12 to 15
Aluminium Wire Rectangular Frame	38 to 41
Aluminium Wire Sphere	70 to 72
Back Cover	76
Blank	2
Blank	75
Circular Open Rustic Wire Armature	60 to 63
Circular Rustic Wire Mechanic with Woven Typha	20 to 23
Coiled Aluminium Ring with Domed Aluminium Mechanic	52 to 53
Crescent Aluminium Frame	58 to 59
From the Author and Coming Soon	74
Front Cover	1
Fruit Net Mechanic	64 to 65
Heart Frame	24 to 27
Index	73
Introduction	4 to 5
Legal	3
Pot Tape Grid	10 to 11
Radial Rustic Wire Armature	6 to 9
Raised Ring Grid	46 to 49
Square Aluminium Wire Armature	54 to 57
Stacked Cornus Square Grid	16 to 19
The Hazards of Using Chicken Wire as a Mechanic.	42 to 45
Threaded Carnations	66 to 69
Triangular Frame of Cornus and Spiralled Aluminium Wire	50 to 51
Wire Armature for Vertical Designs	28 to 31
"Z" Shaped Cornus Frame	32 to 35

Further information on flower arranging books by Gill McGregor can be found at
www.gillmcgregor.com/books
Gill also provides free flower arranging video lessons when you visit
www.gillmcgregor.com/free

From the Author

As our mechanics change, our flower arrangement skills develop to increase our repertoire of designing, arranging and further developing expertise in the art of floral design. The aim of this book is to assist floral artists, teachers, demonstrators and florists and to encourage your own personal design skills and exploration of the use of different materials and techniques to create an even greater range of design styles and mechanics.

Since writing this book and "How to …Go Greener Flower Arranging Leaf Manipulation as a mechanic and in compositions & Cone and Bark Sculptures" I have developed a host of additional mechanics and design ideas using leaf manipulation and hand made structures and armatures.

Volume 2 of "How to …Go Greener Flower Arranging Leaf Manipulation as a mechanic and in compositions &………" well that is our secret soon to be unveiled and will be available in the summer of 2020.

So enjoy the exploration of Floral Art. Happy flower arranging.

Flower Arranging Books written by Gill McGregor include:

- '50 Techniques Used in Contemporary Floral Designs'
  ISBN 978-0-9929332-0-3
- 'How to.. Contemporary Floral Design - Wire Manipulation'
  ISBN 978-0-9929332-1-0
- 'How to - Festive Winter Floral Designs'
  ISBN 978-0-9929332-2-7
- 'How to .. Make—Living Vases, Screens & Structures for Contemporary Floral Designs'
  ISBN 978-0-9929332-3-4
- 'How to .. Apply The Elements & Principles of Floral Design ' - My Little Black Book
  ISBN 978-0-9929332-4-1

'How to.. Go Greener Flower Arranging: Leaf Manipulation and Bark and Cone Structures - Volume 1'
ISBN 978-0-9929332-6-5